OUTBREAK!

BLACK DEATH

KENNY ABDO

Fly!
An Imprint of Abdo Zoom
abdobooks.com

abdobooks.com

Published by Abdo Zoom, a division of ABDO, P.O. Box 398166, Minneapolis, Minnesota 55439. Copyright © 2021 by Abdo Consulting Group, Inc. International copyrights reserved in all countries. No part of this book may be reproduced in any form without written permission from the publisher. Fly!™ is a trademark and logo of Abdo Zoom.

Printed in the United States of America, North Mankato, Minnesota.
102020
012021

Photo Credits: Alamy, Granger Collection, Newscom, Science Source, Shutterstock
Production Contributors: Kenny Abdo, Jennie Forsberg, Grace Hansen
Design Contributors: Dorothy Toth, Neil Klinepier, Laura Graphenteen

Library of Congress Control Number: 2020910919

Publisher's Cataloging-in-Publication Data

Names: Abdo, Kenny, author.
Title: Black death / by Kenny Abdo
Description: Minneapolis, Minnesota : Abdo Zoom, 2021 | Series: Outbreak! |
    Includes online resources and index.
Identifiers: ISBN 9781098223267 (lib. bdg.) | ISBN 9781098223960 (ebook)
    ISBN 9781098224318 (Read-to-Me ebook)
Subjects: LCSH: Black Death--Juvenile literature. | Bubonic plague--Juvenile
    literature. | Epidemics--Juvenile literature. | Epidemics--History--Juvenile
    literature. | Plague--History--Juvenile literature.
Classification: DDC 614.49--dc23

TABLE OF CONTENTS

Black Death 4

Symptoms....................... 8

Source 10

Outbreak! 14

Glossary 22

Online Resources 23

Index 24

BLACK DEATH

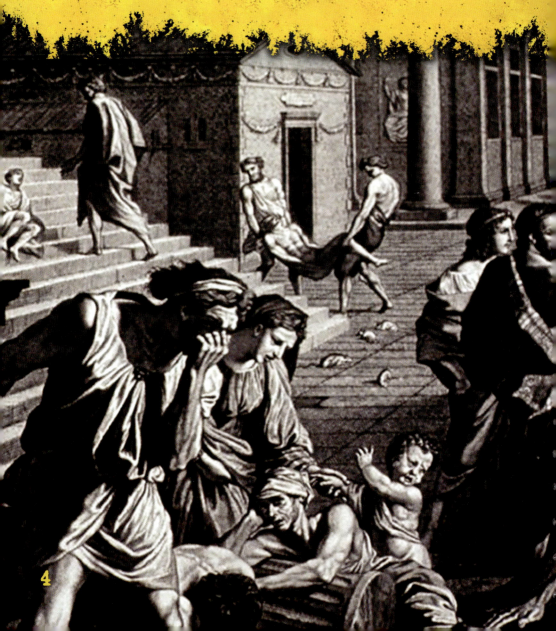

Life during the **Middle Ages** was hard enough. Then, for seven miserable years, the Black Death spread across Europe and Asia.

The Black Death was a **pandemic** of the bubonic **plague**. It single-handedly wiped out more than half of Europe's population.

SYMPTOMS

Those sick with the **plague** experience fever, chills, and seizures. They also have swollen **lymph nodes**. The swelling appears through the skin. The bumps are called "buboes."

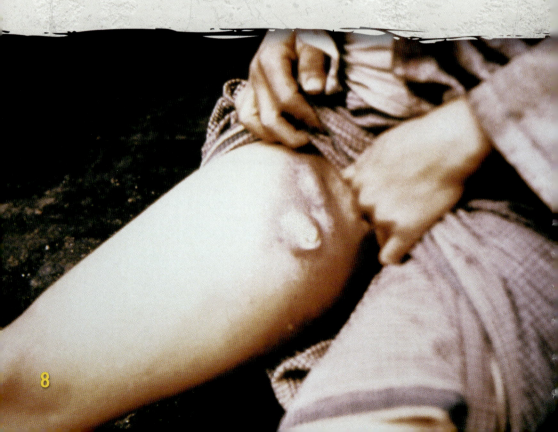

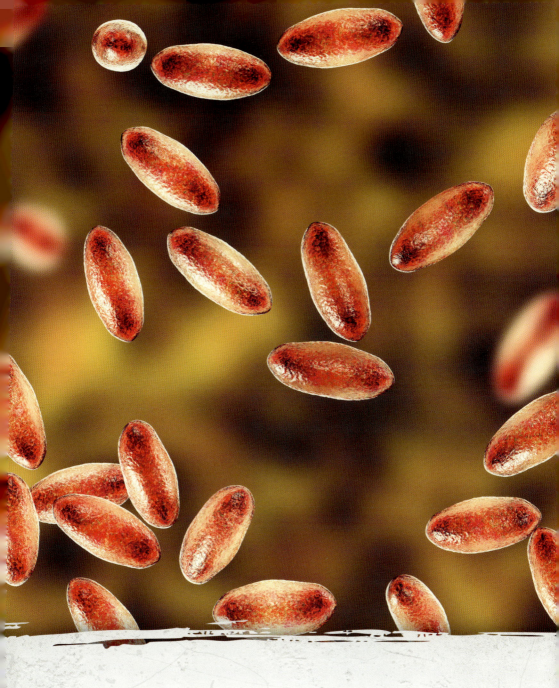

The **plague** bacteria can move easily from human to human through fluids, tissue, and **droplets** in the air.

SOURCE

Y. pestis is the bacteria that causes the **plague**. Fleas and rodents are carriers.

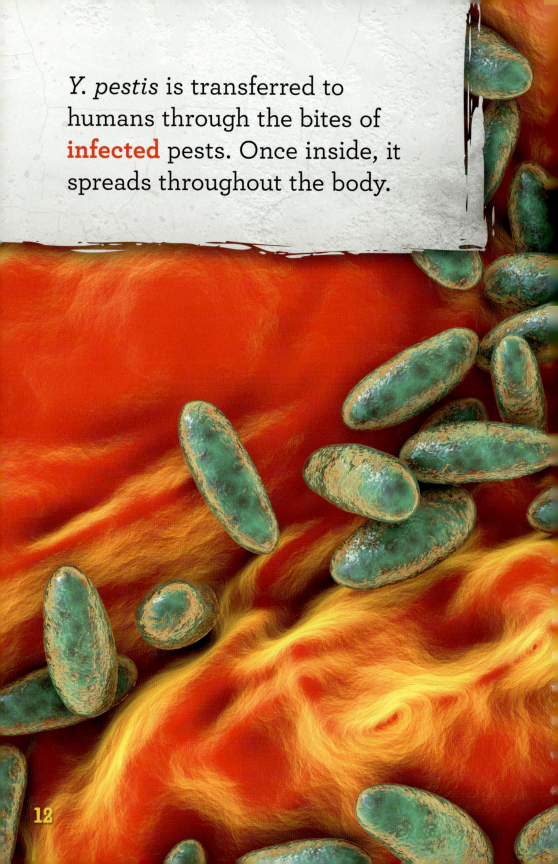

Y. pestis is transferred to humans through the bites of **infected** pests. Once inside, it spreads throughout the body.

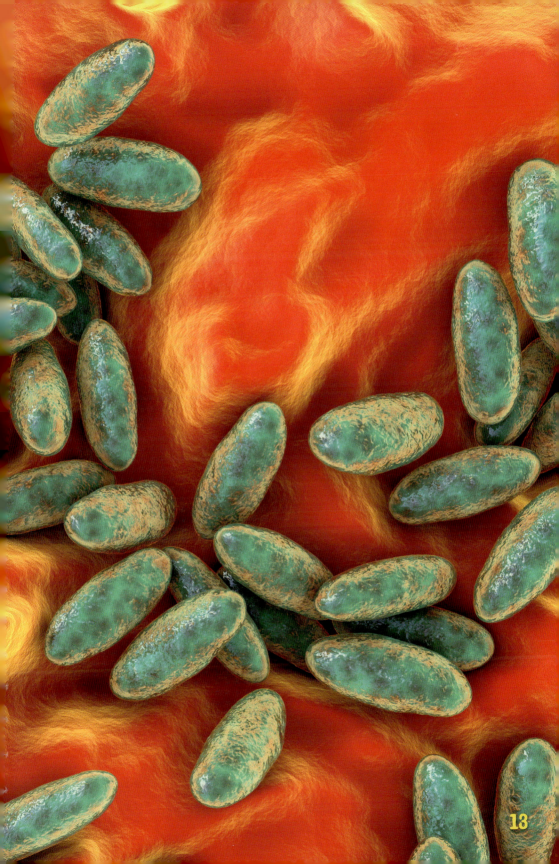

OUTBREAK!

The **plague** arrived in Europe in October 1347. A dozen ships from the Black Sea docked at the Sicilian port of Messina.

Most sailors aboard those ships were dead. Those still alive were fatally ill. They were covered in oozing black boils. Rats and fleas were also onboard.

The Black Death spread quickly. The illness worked quickly, too. A healthy person would go to bed at night and be dead by morning.

People of the time did not understand what diseases were or how they spread. Many believed it was punishment for their sins.

To slow the spread, sailors returning from **infected** areas were held on ships for 30 days. This was called a *trentino*. Later, the time was upped to 40 days and was known as a *quarantino*.

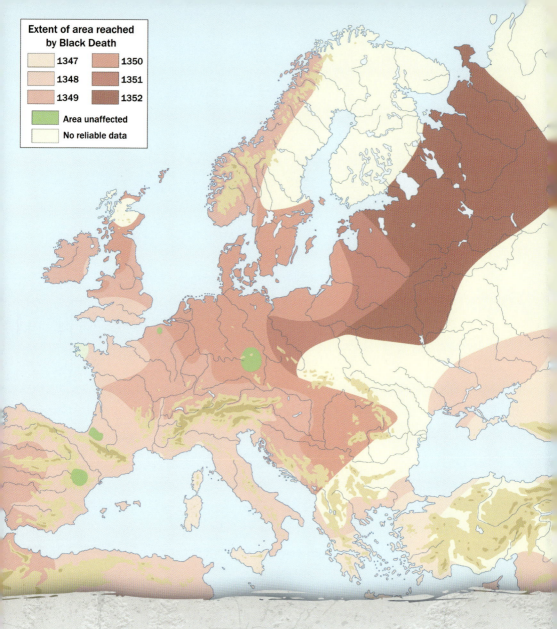

In just seven years, the **plague** killed millions of people across Europe, Asia, and Africa. It would take Europe 200 years to recover the population it lost to the Black Death.

Modern **sanitation** and public-health practices slowed down the **plague**. Still, the World Health Organization (WHO) reports 1,000 to 3,000 cases of it every year.

GLOSSARY

droplets – produced when an infected person talks, coughs, or sneezes. Can spread a disease.

infect – to spread germs or disease to.

lymph nodes – located throughout the body, a bean-shaped structure that helps the body fight infection.

Middle Ages – a period in European history that lasted from about 500 CE to about 1500 CE.

pandemic – a disease that afflicts many people over a vast area.

plague – a bacterial disease that is highly contagious and is caused by *Y. pestis* bacteria.

sanitation – the practice of keeping the public healthy by providing clean living conditions.

ONLINE RESOURCES

To learn more about the Black Death, please visit **abdobooklinks.com** or scan this QR code. These links are routinely monitored and updated to provide the most current information available.

23

INDEX

Asia 5

Europe 5, 7, 14

fleas 10, 15

rats 10, 15

religion 17

signs 8

spread 9, 10, 12, 14, 16, 20

treatments 19, 21

World Health Organization (WHO) 21

Y. pestis 10, 12